Excavators

by Charles Lennie

ABDO
CONSTRUCTION MACHINES
Kids

www.abdopublishing.com

Published by Abdo Kids, a division of ABDO, P.O. Box 398166, Minneapolis, Minnesota 55439.

Copyright © 2015 by Abdo Consulting Group, Inc. International copyrights reserved in all countries. No part of this book may be reproduced in any form without written permission from the publisher.

Printed in the United States of America, North Mankato, Minnesota.

052014

092014

Photo Credits: Shutterstock, Thinkstock

Production Contributors: Teddy Borth, Jennie Forsberg, Grace Hansen

Design Contributors: Candice Keimig, Laura Rask, Dorothy Toth

Library of Congress Control Number: 2013952432

Cataloging-in-Publication Data

Lennie, Charles.

 Excavators / Charles Lennie.

  p. cm. -- (Construction machines)

ISBN 978-1-62970-019-9 (lib. bdg.)

Includes bibliographical references and index.

1. Excavation--Juvenile literature. 2. Construction equipment--Juvenile literature. I. Title.

629.225--dc23

                 2013952432

Table of Contents

Excavators 4

Excavator Parts 8

Different Kinds. 14

More Facts 22

Glossary 23

Index 24

Abdo Kids Code. 24

Excavators

Excavators are used in many ways. They are mainly used for digging.

They are also used

to lift heavy objects.

7

Excavator Parts

Excavators have a few main parts. The driver sits in the **cab**. The controls are in the cab.

8

cab

boom

arm

bucket

9

The **boom** holds the arm.

The arm holds the bucket.

They do the digging.

11

Some excavators move on wheels. Others move on **tracks**.

13

Different Kinds

A **backhoe** loader has two jobs. It can dig and it can load.

14

15

There are **compact** excavators.

They work well in small spaces.

17

There are giant excavators.

They are used to fill giant

dump trucks.

There are **demolition** excavators. They do not have a bucket. They have a special part instead.

21

More Facts

- The biggest excavators are made to fill giant dump trucks that can hold 360 tons (326,587 kg).

- Hybrid excavators are becoming popular. They use up to 25% less fuel in a standard job.

- Crawler excavators are used for the biggest jobs. They are very stable and powerful.

Glossary

backhoe – a machine with a bucket that is used for digging.

boom – a long beam that holds the arm. The boom and arm lift and guide the bucket.

cab – where the driver sits to control the machine.

compact – made to be small in size to work in smaller spaces.

demolition – to tear down.

track – continuous metal band around the wheels of a heavy vehicle.

Index

arm 10

backhoe 14

boom 10

bucket 10, 20

cab 8

controls 8

dig 4, 10, 14

driver 8

dump trucks 18

lift 6

tracks 12

wheels 12

abdokids.com

Use this code to log on to abdokids.com and access crafts, games, videos and more!

Abdo Kids Code:
CEK0199